A BABY BOOMERS HISTORY OF GUILDERLAND, NY

1950's – 1980's

FRENCH'S HOLLOW - 1957

A BABY BOOMERS HISTORY OF GUILDERLAND, NY

1950's – 1980's

To all of my friends in from
Guilderland, NY

Based on the website and contributors:

http://www.myfambly.com/GLD1H.html

For more information:
www.jgreenbooks.com

CONTENTS

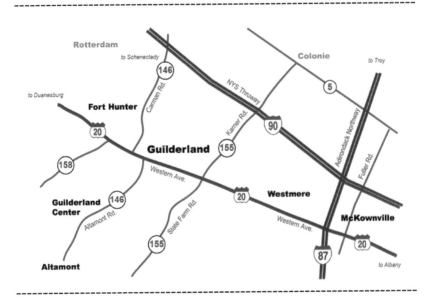

This simplified map shows the town of Guilderland and the major areas covered in this book as indicated in the table of contents. The photographs in this book are reproduced in black and white for economy of printing. For color versions, please go to the website. It is however, the author's opinion that black and white photos enhance, rather than detract from, the vintage nature of the narrative.

One of the purposes of this book is to preserve and augment the website, *which will no doubt cease to exist when this author does* for lack of maintenance and funding. It is my hope that you enjoy this brief trip down memory lane as much as I did creating the website and this book.

INTRODUCTION

Faded photographs, covered now with lines and creases, tickets torn if half, memories of times and places...

The town of Guilderland has a long, rich history dating even before its incorporation in 1803. This well documented. For those interested, *Images of America – Guilderland, NY* - From Arcadia Publishing. Alice Begley and Mary Ellen Johnson is a good read.

For the baby boomer generation however, the town holds a different history, not covered in any textbook. We did not consider it history at the time because we were living in it. Places we lived, loved, learned, worked and played, taken for granted, as though nothing would ever change. Those days from the 1950's to 1980's, were times of great change, not only in the culture of America, but also as reflected in the town.

The town of Guilderland, a mostly rural suburb coupled with the hamlet of Guilderland Center and the village of Altamont, nestled quietly between Albany and Schenectady. McKownville, Westmere, and the eastern part of the hamlet of Guilderland proper, closest to Albany saw the first rise in housing developments. The Fort Hunter area because of its proximity to Rotterdam and Schenectady was similar. Altamont was, and still is, a self-contained village. The town was just beginning to move into full suburban mode. Crowing roosters, farmer's fields, roadside stands, empty fields, streams and woods soon replaced by ice cream shops, diners, bowling alleys, bars, burger joints, housing developments and schools. To coin a phrase, it might have been be called – "Burbrural."

Like much of history, it didn't last long. Pictorial evidence is scarce. What little there is resides in old photo albums or shoeboxes. And in this book. The day of digital images from cameras, phones or tablets was decades away. Who gave any thought to snapping a photo of Carvel, Frosty, The Penguin or Dutcher's ice cream? We ate, drank and caroused at Fonda's, Hopper's, Tommy Polito's, Dell's, The Late 'n' Lazy or the Village Drummer. Take photos? – no way.

Friends or relatives might stay at the Country Squire Motel, Bailey's Cabins, The Tom Sawyer Motor Inn, the Governors Motor Inn or the M&M Motel. A quick bite to eat was often at the Bumble Bee, Will Roy, Mike's Diner or Walt's Subs. Finer, more expensive fare found at The Altamont Manor, The Bavarian Chalet, The Shadow Box, Howard Johnson or Harry's Beef Bottle and Beer.

Lazy summer days were whiled away at McKown's Grove, Tawasentha Park or French's Hollow. We saved money to go to the Altamont Fair in August.

We bought our groceries at Spinosa's, Gruelichs, Star Market or the A&P. We filled our tanks and got our oil checked at Joe's Service Station, O'Hanlon's or P.L. Turnpike Yattaw Esso. Other needs satisfied by Robert Hall, Western Auto, Robinson & Hennett Hardware, Ted & Marions Sporting Goods, Candy Kraft or Master Cleaners.

**

It was the place that we *lived, learned, loved, worked and played*. And not always in that order. Our parents, part of the "greatest generation," were as varied in their occupations as our grandparents - laborers, farmers, business people, clerks, teachers, house wives, or professionals. Some of us were poor. Some of us were wealthy. Most of us were some place in between.

We lived in tiny houses, apartments (of which there were few), farmhouses, trailers, suburban developments, on lonely rural roads and in a few cases, mansions. For the most part however, we all learned in the same place. Depending geographically where we lived, we attended Altamont, Fort Hunter, Westmere or Guilderland Elementary Schools - kindergarten through sixth grade. Pre-school was rare, although some, like the author, went to Happy Day Nursery School. Before the advent of the Farnsworth Middle School, we moved on (not graduated) to Junior High School in Guilderland Center adjacent to Guilderland Central High School. Our teachers, we loved, hated or tolerated. Often said, with some sense of accuracy, is that we remember many of our teachers, (mostly the good ones), but all of our coaches, good or bad. Our educations varied. Some of us dropped out, some went to work directly from high school, while others went on to college and beyond.

At various times in school we also found love. Elementary school often had its share of crushes or puppy loves. Can you remember that little girl or cute boy who first made your heart go pitter pat?

Later in high school, love or lust took a more serious turn, sometimes with disastrous consequences - family conflicts or an unplanned pregnancy. Once, in a while, we found our first, and sometimes last, spouses in our high school sweethearts. Some of us never found love later in life, some found many lovers. Regardless of outcome, most of us had a brush or two with love in school.

Most of us learned about work outside of school and family at this time. After school, or summer jobs with local businesses often left lasting impressions. Punching a register, pumping gas, planting crops, slinging hash, stocking shelves, working construction, grounds maintenance, or waiting tables, we learned the value of a dollar. Dollars put down on our first car or put away for college - *sometimes both*. In many cases, our relationships with our employers formed fond memories. In some cases, not so much but we learned about life as we worked.

How we played changed as we aged. We played inside or outside and often brought the dirt of the back yard or woods with us inside much to our parent's dismay. Tree houses or doll houses, and often both. School playgrounds, the neighbor's back yard or basement were our playgrounds. We played pick-up football or baseball games and board games instead of computer games. This sometimes moved on to high school sports teams or the chess club. We went to Tawasentha Park, McKowns Grove, The Thunderbird, French's Hollow or the Normans Kill to picnic or swim. We discovered nature in the fields, woods, streams and farms nearby. We graduated from tricycles to bicycles to motorcycles. We moved from playing with toy cars, finding abandoned cars in the woods to driving and tinkering with cars. We watched bowling on *TV Tournament Time* with Howard Tupper, sometimes to start bowling at Town & Country or Westlawn Lanes. From playing with sticks and toy guns, we sometimes learned to hunt and fish from our parents or older siblings. Some of us joined the military or drafted for Vietnam. Caroline's Railroad thrilled us as little kids and as did roller coasters, the spider or the scrambler at The Altamont Fair when we got old enough. For many the Fair was the high point of entertainment in August.

We lived, learned, loved, worked, played *and then we moved on.* Some have stayed in town or nearby but we have also moved to every state in America and every continent on the planet, from remote wilderness to the wilds of immense urban areas.

***

Few pictures were taken at the time, because little thought was put into these and many other places that filled our lives and memories. We were busy living our lives or preparing for our lives later on. We took it for granted that icons of our youth would never change – *if we gave it any thought at all.*

If photos are scarce, memories, stories and anecdotes remain. The photos and stories in this book, have been gathered from many sources. Some from the author's personal archives, others from the Facebook page – *You know you're from Guilderland when...* Many are from people, like the author, who grew up in town and in some cases still reside there or nearby. Those persons credited for their submissions and listed in the appendix.

Photos may fade but memories remain intact - *for the most part.*

Please enjoy the walk...

GUILDERLAND

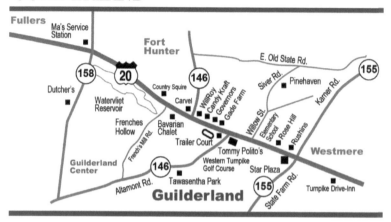

This chapter covers the hamlet of Guilderland itself as roughly shown on the map above. Most businesses old and new are along US Route 20. At that time, housing also followed the routes shown although much was up Willow Street and its tributaries. New developments started near McCormack's corners down Okara and Highland Drive as well as Altamont and Carman Roads.

HARTMAN'S CORNERS

The Hartman House

Hartman's Corners, at the junction of Altamont Road (rt. 146) and US 20, is the official designation. The corner has also been known as, Fonda's Corners, Polito's Corners and currently Stewart's Corners. The historic Hartman house and family gave it the name originally, but the two taverns were popular choices for a long time. The Hartman House, shown above, built in the late 1800s gave the corner its original name. Its masonry construction was classic for the time. The author was often in and around the house. Renovations revealed that it was at one time, used as a post office because of the post office boxes found behind a wall. A cannon ball sat on the front porch for many years, according to the residents -- found embedded in a wall!

The house was demolished in 1960 to make way for a Texaco station which itself was demolished later for Stewart's. The last known residents were the Servin family with their children Darlene (Dolly) and Jeff. They also raised and groomed Kerry Blue Terriers.

The photo of this two story red brick house (above left), taken in 2017, but except for the satellite dish is essentially unchanged. It was the Turnpike Motel. The room units that were on the left are long gone. Several hundred yards away to the east stands a house that except for the portico and wood construction is nearly the same design as the Hartman house that was diagonally across the corner where a Stewart's Shop now stands.

Above also taken in 2017 - The house on the left is just south on the west side of the corner on rt. 146 and is just as it was years ago. Donny Brown lived there for a time. To the right is the house that "Pop" Carpenter lived in. He was an old farmer that sold his produce at Pop's Road stand. (altered considerably)

U. S. ROUTE 20 - GUILDERLAND, N. Y.

There seems to be some confusion and controversy about the above old photos.

FROM FACEBOOK "Albany the way it was": Fonda's Cabins & Restaurant was located at or near the intersection of Routes 20 and 146 and operated from around 1938-1962. In 1967, Guilderland entrepreneur Charles Bohl, applied to operate the then-abandoned cabins as efficiency apartments, but denied, as all units were less than the required 720 square feet. I had originally asked you where exactly was this, when was it torn down, and what's there now, and you came through in spades. For the record, it was where Tommy Polito's used to be, and actually became Polito's, as the cabins were moved elsewhere – the Southeast corner of the intersection. – *Al Quaglieri*

From Don Albright (lifelong resident and town employee):
Actually, there is nothing there. It was Polito's. The cabins were moved to the site of Karner Psychological, which was the Castle D'or Hotel. The cabins were joined together to form the motel.

The author, who lived less than 300 yards from the intersection from 1957-1984, has a different opinion.

FONDA'S
Cor. Western Turnpike and Altamont Road
ROUTE 20 — GUILDERLAND, N. Y.
"Where Good Friends Meet"
BILL MATTICE AND HIS HOT MUSIC
FRIDAY — SATURDAY — SUNDAY NITES
GOOD FOOD—CHOICE BEVERAGES

Fonda's Grill and Tavern adjacent to a historic house that the Fonda's (*including Don Fonda whom the author and his brother Vilko knew*) occupied the corner until Tommy Polito bought it and turned it into Tommy Polito's Tavern an area icon for over two decades. At the time, there no traffic light on the corner. It had only a yellow caution blinker. Directly to the south was a small strip of apartment units occupied at least until 1969, as I knew a boy and his mother who lived in one them. Adjacent to Polito's

Tavern was a barbershop. First, it was Roy's and later, Joe's barber shop. Both barbers cut the authors hair.

Tommy, known as the singing bartender, was well loved, by his friends and customers. Whether singing a tune or giving the women a flower, he was friendly, outgoing and knew how to treat his friends and customers. In the late afternoon, it was a working man's place, to stop and have a brew or two after work. At night, the place became a popular hangout for the younger set with quarter beers and an old jukebox cranking out the music. The Italian style checked tablecloths and red candles saw countless pizzas, sandwiches and drinks. Class reunions for Guilderland High School often started and ended at Tommy's. The slogan on his matchbook read: "A friendly place, where friends meet."

A New Year's Eve at Tommy Polito's Tavern:

Four of us were double dating on New Years Eve in 1970- John Green, Paul Gardner, Debbie Gogol and Nancy George. Having gone to several places that were private parties or had high cover charges, we decided to stop at Polito's to have a drink and figure out what to do next. *We never left.* We knew almost everyone in the place and prices were the same as always. Around 11:00, Tommy's people started putting all sorts of food on some side tables – including pizzas, rolls, roast beef, turkey, cheese and ham. After all the food was set out Tommy turned off the jukebox just long enough to announce -- "The food is on the house - so dig in - and Happy New Year!" *- John Green - GCHS class of 1971*

The backside of Polito's c. 1970s

Tommy was in the habit of sleeping next door at the old house if he closed up late. One morning, he didn't wake up. Many people including his bartenders opened up the place after the funeral. Since Tommy's liquor license expired with him, the drinks were free. The Fonda house, was dismantled and moved to an historic village in New England. The Tavern was razed. Only the memories and a vacant lot remain as of this writing.

A traffic accident in front of Polito's

Authors note: this little ditty was written about Tommy Polito's Tavern
and goes to the tune of: "Those were the days my friend"
-by Mary Hopkins:

"The Tommy Polito's song"

Once upon a time, there was a tavern
Tommy Polito's was its name
We all gathered there when still in high school,
Growing up was very far away...

There were the quarter brews and a fight or two
we'd drink and talk all the long night through
There was a smooch or two and then another brew
'cause we were young and old was far away.

We were way too young to get a drink then
they'd just wink and look the other way
But what did it matter to us back when
we'd get served as long as we could pay!

There were the quarter brews and a kiss or two
we knew 'most everyone by name
There was a fight or two and then another brew
'cause we were young and old was far away.

We all had our plans that was for certain
career and adventure maybe more
but they were behind a distant curtain
all we had back then was what we wore

We'd have a drink or two maybe some smooching too
we'd feed the juke with quarters all night long
There'd be a fight or two but then another brew
'cause we were young and old was far away.

We have all gone our different ways now
the tavern torn down so long ago
Tommy himself is in his grave now
along with the memories we all knew.

We'd have a drink or two maybe a kiss who knew
we'd feed the juke with quarters all night long
there was a fight or two and then another brew
'cause we were young and old was far away.

When I look back with much nostalgia
what little I knew when I was young
would be nice to know what I know now
back when I was so very dumb

I'd have a drink or two maybe another too
I new most everyone by name
break up a fight or two and have another brew
'cause I was young and old was far away.

PONDERING POLITIO'S*

SIDE BAR: Dan Nieliwocki, owner of The Village Drummer, sent the author a note that in essence said that although he and Tommy were technically competitors they were also good friends, often helping each other out if one or the other ran out of something. He was deeply saddened when Tommy died alone in the house next door to the tavern.

I came in the back door and plopped down on a red covered bar stool. Plenty to choose from too, it was only four o'clock in the afternoon and the place was empty – well almost.

Tommy was at the other end of the bar talking to Frank. He put one finger up to me, meaning hold on a second, said something to Frank that I couldn't hear and came down to where I was sitting. "Bud draft?" he asked, but he already had the glass in his hand. Quarter drafts were the standard and he saw that I had a stack of quarters in front of me. Frank, in his usual "working man's" clothes, complete with a nametag sewn on the breast pocket of his blue shirt, and baggy matching chinos, was nursing one at the other end of the bar. He was the only other customer. I just nodded and smiled at Tommy and pushed a quarter out.

When it was slow in the afternoons Tommy tended bar. The place had what I always thought of as a split personality. Older guys like Frank stopped by after work for a beer or two but were mostly gone by the time the younger crowd started coming in.

"Thanks," I said as Tommy brought the beer over and put a coaster under it.

Just then, the back door opened and a big burly, long-haired dude walked in. Long hair did *not* look like he was in a good mood.

"You know you're not welcome in here!" Tommy said loudly and in an angry tone, I rarely heard from this generally good-natured man. "Go on – get out!"

"F**k you Tommy!" the dude hollered and walked right out.

"What's that all about Tommy?" I asked.

"Kicked that guy out last week for fighting and swearing up a storm and told him never to come back," Tommy responded. "This is a friendly place where friends meet," Tommy said as he picked up a book of matches, "you see, it says so right here on my matchbooks."

Tommy started gliding down the walkway behind the bar in his usual way. For a heavy-set portly man he was light on his feet and had a happy walk. Suddenly there was a screech of tires out front. A moment later, the door was flung wide and left open as the long-haired dude came in fuming and cursing. The stream of invectives was loud and long, ending with a comment about Tommy's parentage and an invitation to perform sodomy on him. While this was going on, Frank just sat staring at his beer. The dude was still standing in the doorway. "You stupid fat f**k..." was all he managed to get out of his mouth when Frank got off his stool as quick as a pro linebacker sacking a quarterback, grabbed the man by his collar and crotch, and lifted him up like a sack of potatoes. Frank carried him out the door and flung him across the hood of his yellow car, snapping the aerial of as he fell off the other side and landed in the dirt. Never saying a word, Frank closed the door gently, and returned to his stool calmly and took a sip of his beer. We all listened as the car started loudly, and peeled out of the front parking lot, spitting dirt and gravel.

Tommy pulled a fresh draft, walked it down and said quietly, "Thanks Frank."

Frank just nodded and took another sip.

A big fellow came in and sat next to me. It had been a few years, like since junior high school, but I recognized Butch instantly. Harold, a.k.a. "Butch" Warner was one of the toughest sons of bitches I ever knew. Some my friends had bad blood with him when we were kids, but for some reason Butch liked me and never made any trouble with me, which didn't exactly, break my heart. It was always good thing to have a tough guy on your side if the shit hit the fan with the local bullies.

I asked him how he was doing.

"Okay, just working - just stopped in for a beer." Butch was never one for eloquence but this was unusually low key, even for him. He looked down, either something was bugging him or he had mellowed out a bit. I sure as hell wasn't going to ask. Guys like Butch are not much for sharing their troubles and not likely to ever be seen in a family counselor's office, so we just sat next to each other for a while, saying nothing.

 A short time later, a hard, cranky looking fellow came in, walked up to Butch and shoved him a little. "You're an asshole, Butch," he said without even a hello. "Everyone thinks you're all tough, but I think you're a pussy!" Butch ignored him and just went on with his beer.

I thought this was unusual, but slid my bar stool over a foot or two, just in case and waited for the eruption. The moron's tirade continued unabated with no effect other than eliciting from Butch, "Hey, just having a beer here. Don't want no trouble." By this time, a few others including the night bartender took notice but the guy just kept at it, trying everything short of a punch to rile Butch up. Butch just sat and drank his beer and ordered another.

"Put his beer on my tab," I told the bartender, then turned to Butch and said, "for old time sake." The tension was thick, especially for anyone who knew Butch.

"Yeah, thanks," he said softly.

The troublemaker, feeling many eyes on him, and not any very sympathetic to a man bent on getting a one way ticket to the nearest emergency room. He finally said, "F**k it," and walked out the back door. Nothing else was said, so I finished my drink, said goodbye to Butch and went home feeling surprised, puzzled and relieved all at the same time. – *J. Green*

---

*excerpted in part from *"Tommy Polito's Tavern"* – another book by the author.

I can remember Tommy standing behind the bar singing one particular night. I think it was around St Patrick's Day and it was Danny boy or something along those lines but I remember that Tommy had a hell of a great singing voice! I always loved Polito's, red and white checked tablecloths, and pitchers of beer. It was really the social hub of Guilderland for many of us.
- *John LaJeunesse*

Included in this section is Andrews Trailer Court because of its proximity to the corner. Mr. Andrews owned the court and had two large greenhouses in which he grew flowers to sell. He also landscaped the court with them. Petunias, pansies and geraniums, planted to beautify the court. They even adorned the "wash house," a plain green cinderblock building that housed the water pumps, holding tanks, washing machines, restrooms and the mailroom. He also provided clothes lines for drying laundry and 50-gallon steel barrels he called incinerators for burning trash. A point, not a regular well, supplied the water. Occasionally he would walk around with a forked stick or "divining rod" to find water. When the stick bent down he told old Zeke or young Ray Kipp, to drive a point in the ground to provide water for the court.

For the most part, it was tenanted by retirees or working people. It had been planned for small trailers, and there were hook-ups for travel trailers passing through. The term "mobile home" hadn't been invented yet. Most were 8 feet wide by 35 to 45 feet long. Generally well kept and landscaped nicely. Since the trailers were only 15 feet apart, arranged in a rough oval around which ran a gravel one-lane driveway, people got to know their neighbors pretty quickly.

The court in 1957 – the authors home third from the left

The oldest remaining trailer once belonged to Maude Couchman.

There were the Uhl's on the corner. Hugh and Irene McGaughan lived across from them. Old Mrs. Zimmerman and Mrs. Tatreault mostly kept to themselves. Ruth Unright had a Boston terrier, which she plied with beer until it staggered. There was Ted and Josephine Murch. Ted was a chiropractor and childhood friend of the author's father. Josephine helped him in his office on Albany Street and took care of the two Laundromats they owned. Next to them, old Maude Couchman and her cat, Bing. Around the bend just off the oval lived Mary Johnson and Mary Lynch - working women who lived together and were always referred to simply as "The Mary's." Next to them was Fred Carpenter who had a stiff leg from an auto accident and always had tiny sports cars sitting next to his place. Along the back of the oval were the Schultz's, the Robert's and Smith's. Don Snyder and Don Kline, both Guilderland teachers lived in the court for a while. Mrs. Anna Ogsbury lived near the corner and eventually sold her trailer to Josephine Murch after Ted died. Charlie and Emma Scrafford lived just off the oval, and he and his wife were very jovial folks. Lastly, across from the Scrafford's, was old Mr. Willet. Twylla Schell was his granddaughter. He drove a little blue Ford Falcon and had a neatly trimmed white moustache.

The author of this book lived there from 1957-1984. On a visit to town in 2011, a current resident opined that he knew all about the court having lived there for ten years. His jaw dropped when told of my tenure, awaking to the sound of roosters from the chicken coops on the farm behind. Alex Carpenter's grandparents owned the farm and chicken coops. They also ran the previously mentioned, "Pop's Road Stand" - a place for fresh produce in season, candy, cigarettes and ice cream and only a short walk through the woods or fields from the court. Old "Pop" worked the fields while "Grandma" sat in an old white Adirondack chair knitting or sewing.

As time passed, larger and larger trailers were added inside and around the perimeter of the oval. The oiled gravel driveway paved over. When Mr. Andrews died, ownership passed to his son-in law, Al Dwyer, who in time sold it to Gene Budini.

Above: The court after a winter storm c. 1960.
The author's mother sunbathing in the yard -
As you can see, "yards" were tiny.

MOVING WEST ON WESTERN

The Gade Farm, on Western Avenue, has been family owned and operated since 1878. Barely visible except for the family homes in the 1960s, it has expanded over the years to include retail sales.

The photos above: 1. Left is the sign today. 2. Top right the original Gade home on the north side of US 20 – Structurally unstable, it was torn down years ago. 3. Middle right - The newer Gade home, directly opposite which has not changed much. John "Grandpa" Gade lived there. The author knew grandson Peter Gade. We played and caught the school bus together while watching Grandpa John cross to the farm when US 20 was only two lanes and lightly travelled in the 1960's. Bottom right – John (Jack) Gade inside before his passing and his son Jim Gade who as of this writing now runs the family business. The farm extends deep north of US 20 and the family owns a goodly stretch of property extending to Hartman's Corners.

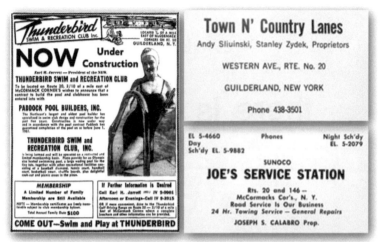

Newspaper ad and business cards - Note the phone number's exchange.

The Thunderbird Swim & Recreation Club opened in May 1961. It was located behind the Thunderbird Golf Driving Range, which opened in 1959. Miniature golf and archery opened a few years later. The pool was 44,000 square feet, L-shaped and heated, thus open for swimming from May to September. The complex was still operating in 1983.

Adventures beyond the Thunderbird:

On an early October day in the early 70s I went over to Dave Cianis' house on route 20 across from Okara Drive (his dad Hugo was an insurance agent) to go hunting. We cut behind his house, past the putting range and the driving-range up the hill through the Thunderbird Swim Club parking lot and past the tennis courts in back. We then went into the woods by the pig farm and could see the junked cars some distance away. In the woods, we saw hogs rooting around and continued on to an abandoned field behind the flats going towards the Norman's Kill. In the field, we approached a shallow pond/pothole and as we eased around it, we put up some ducks. I don't think they were mallards - some other kind. We fired with our 12 gauges and two birds went down. We rushed over in the high grass and there was not a bird in sight! We searched over and over in patterns and could not find the ducks. I think we both claimed that each of us hit both of them.

During the search, I saw something moving through the grass in front of me and realized it was a cock pheasant. Not wanting to go home empty handed I quickly bagged him. We hated to give up on the ducks so Dave suggested we go to his house, get the young Golden Retriever he was training and let him sniff around the area. We hiked back, got the dog, my truck and drove somewhere close, maybe by the Drahos farm down from Joe's Sunoco. Dave fired a shot to get the dog scenting for a downed bird. The dog almost immediately put up a pheasant, which Dave bagged with a nice angled shot. Note - these were wild pheasants, not escaped tagged ones from Corlous Pheasant Farm. A short while later Penny, the dog, located the two birds in grass we had trampled down right in the middle of where we had been searching, Dave was ecstatic that the young dog had done so well and we were happy with the game.

The next night we had a game dinner my mom fixed. It was delicious! Later that week, Dave bored our girlfriends to tears recounting the story over pizza at Smitty's Tavern in Voorheesvile. I think he's now a guide in North Dakota. --*Jay Mohr*

My best friend, Deb Lockhart Kilcher, lived right next door to the pro shop. We worked at the miniature golf and archery range, handing out the clubs and golf balls but would sneak into the pool at night. We had so much fun playing miniature golf and shooting bows at the archery range but we never got very good at it.

– *Doreen Reinemann*

Candy Kraft is possibly the oldest business in town aside from the Gade Farm. It was established in 1935.

From their website (www.candykraftcandies.com) - When Claude Ball first opened his door to sell handmade candies the fresh cream he used was delivered by horse-drawn wagons. That was in 1935. Now years later, although delivery methods have changed, the same quality ingredients are producing the same quality candies.

Ownership changed in 1958 to a husband-wife team, Loren & Blanche Pratt. In 1973 they hired a Guilderland High School student to work part-time. He (Bob Pikcilingis) apprenticed under Loren for 11 years. Bob and his wife, Donna, bought the business from them in 1984. Their three children, Julie, Brad and Heidi, have grown up in the candy store, helping whenever they could. Their son, Brad, joined the family business full time in 2006. Over the years, the business has maintained its personal touch while growing to serve wholesale markets. We invite you to experience our handmade candy that has captured the palates of many generations.

Brad, Beth & Bob

A VALENTINE MEMORY

An older man in his late fifties with a white beard, stopped into Candy Kraft in the summer of 2011. After chatting with Bob Pikcilingis for a while, he said, "I remember tramping here in the snow one February when I was in the sixth grade to buy a box of candy for a girl I was sweet on for Valentines Day. That was around 1965. She lived down on Highland Drive just a little way from here. I stuck it in her mailbox, no card, no message – was too shy to let her know who sent it. Isn't that stupid?"

Bob replied, "I don't know if it was 'stupid' or not fellow, but back then there was only one girl I know of that lived on Highland Drive. Her name was Sharon Rapsard."

The man responded, "Yeah, that would be right. That would be very right." He bought some candy and left.

Six years later, the man returned to the store. Bob was still there. Harkening back to the Valentines story, he said to Bob, "A couple years ago, I bumped into that girl on Facebook. Her name is Sharon Waldbillig now. She had no clue it was me, but now, over fifty years later she does." He paused and continued, "By the way there was another girl who lived on that street by the name of Roxanne Ballschmieder." - -- *the "old man" was the author.*

The Governors Motor Inn started out as one of the nicest motels in town. Its banquet facility hosted many a wedding reception. Over the years, it degenerated into a sleaze palace with mirrored rooms and the like – probably rooms to rent by the hour too. It partially burned down and parts are still standing as an eyesore as of 2017.

Town 'n' Country Lanes was originally The Turnpike Bowling Alley in the 1950's – 1960's. The business card on a previous page is from 1970. It has been under various ownership and management but is still operating as of 2017. It figures prominently in a story below.

THE VILLAGE DRUMMER

If Tommy Polito's Tavern had a large following, so did the Village Drummer. Some customers patronized both. Some were loyal to only one or the other.

From Carl Burnham: Back in the 1960's it was The Turnpike Lounge. Ralph Carpenter purchased it and the name remained The Turnpike Lounge. Ralph sold to Dan Nieliwocki who turned it into The Village Drummer on June 3, 1974. (*As of the author's visit on 2017, it is now The Pizza Gram*)

One of the funniest stories I can tell is the time we were at the Drummer having a great time and it was the era that streaking was popular. Cliff Francis, Frank Orsini, Charlie Adams and I decided to streak through Town N' Country Lanes. It was the middle of the winter and everyone in the Drummer came out to watch us. We went in the west door by lane one, streaked through the bowling alley and went out the east door by lane 24. Across the street, the crowd cheered us on, but the joke was on us - they locked our clothes in the car. It was a very cold winter night! -- *Ron Furbeck*

I remember a night in mid 1970's, Frank Orsini and Paul Lupien eating – that's right, EATING, beer gasses! I'm proud to call you all my family & friends! Hard to imagine today's generation having the same kind of fun! ---*Jeff Orsini*

They had the best sandwiches for five-dollars. Once a person ordered one, ten more followed. Dan drank coffee and smoked all night long. He never had a drink like many bar owners. When you came in on your birthday, you got a free fireball - on fire. He was a wonderful boss for many years. I was a bartender from 1981-1986. ---*Michelle Morini France*

Dad was married to the bar and everyone was his pal. There didn't seem to be any separation between business and family. That is often how it has to be to be successful - *and he was successful.* Everyone loved my dad! He was also a guy you didn't want to be confronted by if the drink turned you into an a-hole.

He's still a wonderful source of information, a shoulder to cry on and a compassionate, informative confidante. This is a man, who hit a fawn with his truck, got out, and held it in his lap comforting it until it succumbed to its injuries. I understand now having owned my own business for eight years. You gotta live it. Dancing with everyone and the live bands with disco balls and lighted floor made for a truly great experience. I loved to dance. It was like I was in another world. – *Gayle Nieliwocki Gifford*

From Terry Miltner –

I came back from living in Colorado Springs and my brother Gary, was still living with my parents. He was a frequent flyer at both the Drummer and Tommy's. One night after he got out of work we decided to go to the Drummer. When we got there, Dan seemed a little nervous and asked if he could talk to us outside. He asked if I would take over the pool table from the two guys that were strong-arming other patrons. He also mentioned, if we were to get them outside for a fight, he would be indebted to us.

Gary and I were never ones to start a fight in the Drummer but never ran from one either! I put my quarters up and it seemed Dan, who was sitting by the entrance to the kitchen, called my name well before I was due to play. Others squealed but Dan was the owner and most people knew my brother well. I racked them and the guy said they were playing doubles. I said okay but after I win, I'm going to play singles. I beat him without him getting a shot besides the break. He got a little pissed off so I razzed him by saying things like – "my daughter plays a better game."

Dan then tells us to take it outside because he didn't want any trouble inside. I looked at my brother and we both nodded. I told the kid, "What you going to do - shit your pants or are we going outside?" He gets his friend and starts heading for the door. Outside, my brother just cold cocked him and his friend said something stupid like that's not fair! I said, "You didn't read the same rule book as us!" He picked up his friend and left! We went back in and Dan told Michelle, the bartender, "Their beers are free all night!"

From John LaJeunesse -

I brought my brother Tom to the Village Drummer in his wheelchair. Tom had a car accident and broke both legs. I was going to lift Tom up the stairs in his wheelchair and two of his friends were going to lift the back of the chair. I lifted and the chair went right up easily. My mom, all 4'9" of her, would've shot both of us if she knew we where there.

From Kathleen Ashline

I fondly remember Dan Nieiwicki from The Village Drummer. It's unbelievable the stuff he had to put up with from a bunch of drunk kids. He was always so sweet and kind to everyone. I'm sure he won't remember me, but there's a lot of "kids" out here who remember *him* well. The "VD" was one of my favorite spots on the weekend. My ex-husband's band played there a time or two as well. It was always a good time! Every time I go to Pizza Gram those memories come rushing back. God less you, Mr. Nielwocki for giving us those great times! –

From Jim Purtell –

I used to call it "the bar that made Nieliwocki famous."

Note: Some readers may not understand this reference to Schlitz beer – *"Schlitz, the Beer that made Milwaukie famous"* was their advertising slogan for a long time – *editor*

After a few New Years Eves, I decided to try something different due to the expense of the bands. I discussed this idea with my employees about closing on New Years and they were okay with it. So, we closed on New Years Eve and had a Polish New Years Eve the second weekend of January, when the bands were regular price and the buffet we served was also reasonable. I think I charged $5.00. Well, I hit a home run. We were absolutely jammed! My mother-in-law was my lunchtime cook. Every one called her Ma. She set up a real nice big buffet, of course, my wife and I helped to put it all together. We also served a free glass of champagne at midnight. It really turned out to be a great idea and it worked for several more years. - *Dan Nieliwocki*

Dan Nieliwocki

Before this Chapter moves further west to McCormack's Corners, these two old houses are worth mention, both of which have been landmarks on US route 20 for a long time. The inset photo is almost next to Joe's Service station. The main photo shows a house owned by Gary Gillespie, owner of Colonial Acres Nursery.

Joe's Service Station is yet another Guilderland icon. Once a Sunoco station, owned by Joe Calabro, it is currently owned and operated by his son, D.J. Calabro. Anyone who knew Joe, can readily see the family resemblance.

McCORMACK'S CORNERS
US Route 20 (Western Ave.) and Route 146, (Carman Road.)

There is very little pictorial reference of this corner, now occupied by a drug store and a gas station/ convenience store.

At one time, Carvel with a huge vanilla cone on top was on the southwest corner and Frosty Ice Cream was diagonally across sporting a vanilla and chocolate twist cone of equal size. Will Roy, a wooden structure drive-in stood ready with burgers, dogs, fries and some would argue the best fish fry in the state. A variety of bars inhabited the fourth part of the corner including one oddly named "State Fair," and later "Racers."

Slightly north of the corner on Carman Road, was - and still is - The Albany Beverage Corp. A short distance to the west on US Route 20 stood the Country Squire Motel. These places shown above, along with the Corner Ice Cream shop, which was the successor to Carvel.

*****

THE BAVARIAN CHALET

The Bavarian Chalet run by the Zwicklbauer family for decades, closed in 2005. It grew from a soccer-player's clubhouse built on a cow pasture into a fine German restaurant that hosted many functions, including weddings, club meetings, banquets, class reunions, and soccer tournaments. It also featured a small game preserve. The inset photo shows Franz & Erna Zwicklbauer - original owners of the Bavarian Chalet. As of this writing, the Chalet has been torn down - replaced by a community center.

From Anita Thiele-Green – "My father Erich Thiele was the care taker of the Bavarian Chalet for many years. He did everything from bar tending, to mowing the 5-acre property. My mother Charlotte Gerstenberger also worked in the kitchen & my sister Gerda Wright was a waitress for many years as well. I worked checking coats a couple of times. So many great memories! I also had my wedding reception there in 1975."

"We purchased four of their bar stools back in the late 80's for our camp in the Adirondacks –we still use them today! My father was also on their soccer team and was one of the leading scorers."

Wedding photo taken at the Bavarian Chalet.
June of 1975 - Anita and her father Erich.

BAVARIAN CHALET STAFF PHOTOS
-- *courtesy of Rudolf Zwicklbauer*

BAVARIAN STAFF: Wanetta Kisby, Susan Birch, Rita Putnam, Erna Zwicklbauer, my Aunt (Tante) Marie Zwicklbauer Froedtert, Erich Thiele, Mike Hendricks, Charlotte Thiele, Mark Sengenberger (also married a Thiele...Heidi) and Jimmy Hendricks.

Helene Zwicklbauer, Elfriede Mays (worked for my parents for about 30 years), cousin Werner Zwicklbauer, Billy Wright (Anita's brother in law), Erna, ???? a local boy, Tante Marie.

Young Rudolf Zwicklbauer –
everyone who ever ate at the Bavarian remembers the paintings.

*****

I grew up on Western Ave. My house sat right in front of the Bavarian Chalet. Across the street was my favorite place to hang out in the summer - Lizzi's Farm Stand. I had my first Orange Crush soda there. It was only a dime. Gus and Jean Lizzi had a son named Cosimo. When we got off the school bus Jean Lizzi always let us pick out a piece of fruit to take home, and would hold our hands as she crossed the street with us. The farm stand is gone now, but every time I bite into a juicy black plum, it reminds me of that magical farm stand called Lizzi's. -- *Leslie Anne LaGuardia*

FRENCH'S HOLLOW

In a long bygone day, French's Mill used the flow of water from the Norman's Kill for manufacturing. When the dam was completed, to for the Watervliet reservoir in 1916, the gently flowing water and deep pools became a popular picnic and swimming area.

French's Mill Road, from which the above photo was taken, has been long closed to road traffic for jurisdictional budgetary reasons and lack of funding for repair. It remains open to foot traffic only and is still a popular walking trail. On the other side of the hollow, the road continues and the house pictured below circa 1830 stands amidst beautiful shaded grounds. The reservoir itself, once a popular fishing place, now closed to that purpose.

Notwithstanding, The Hollow is the one place in the hamlet of Guilderland that remains virtually unchanged over the decades. It was chosen for that reason, to be the central theme of the cover of this book.

SHARP'S CORNERS

The Sharps brothers owned both SW (Lloyd) and SE (Lloyd's brother) sides of Sharp's Corners (Route 158 & US 20) and were just down the hill from Dutcher's Ice Cream. Both houses were grand buildings in their day. We lived up the hill on Western Turnpike. Dad bought our property from Lloyd Sharp. The Sharp family home was once located in the back end of our property before they lost it to fire. The well and the lilac bushes for the old house are visible today.

During the 1950's, Lloyd Sharp the farmer who lived at Sharp's Corner sold eggs and Mom would send my older sister and I to walk down the hill to buy a dozen. If there were too few eggs on hand, he would take us with him into the chicken coup and let us pick up a couple more. It was always a treat to visit him as he would have stories to tell and his wife would always tempt us with her raspberry pie or lemonade. He also would turn our apples into cider. But I was most fascinated by the air raid siren he kept in the barn. During World War II, he was an air raid warden and entrusted with an air raid siren that he kept in his barn. In the 1950's the air raid wardens in the area would run their hand-cranked sirens on 4th of July at noon. I remember hearing multiple sirens on those memorial occasions but the annual running of the sirens stopped in the 1960 as the volunteer fire departments did not want to the sirens to disturb the emergency message/siren system they were developing. *-- Robert Batzinger*

*****

While this house is related to the specific history of my family, the story is very typical of many families that moved into the area after World War II. Like many GI returning from service after the war, Mr. Frank Batzinger quickly married and together with his wife build this house from ground up. This home was built on an experimental apple orchard that Mr. Batzinger purchased in 1948 from Lloyd Sharp (who lived in the farmhouse on the northeast side of Sharp's Corner). The house follows the plans of a brick New English cottage selected from one of many free plans that the US government provided for those taking loans on the GI Bill. Others in the area doing the same form of homesteading giving rise to many local building supply companies. The Batzingers moved in as soon as the basement could be capped off in 1950.

Most of the work was done by Mr Batzinger although I remember that some local contractors were used for special jobs like plumbing and roofing. My siblings and I often assisted by holding flashlights or boards being cut or nailed. The upstairs was added in 1957. My earliest memory at the age of three, was watching the refrigerator raised from the basement by block and tackle. As the family grew, the bedrooms under the dormers were expanded and the children pitched in to dig the basement for the extension to the dining room. A shed was added in the mid 1960's to house the garden tools and equipment.

The family maintained about 1 acre as a vegetable garden that supplied fresh produce in the summer and the resources for the canned and frozen veggies consumed the rest of the year. Fruit and jam came from the apple, peach, pear and cherry trees along with grape, strawberry, raspberry, rhubarb and current patches. Frank was a weekend hunter and fishermen and kept the freezer stocked with a wide variety of meet. This simple house became a very comfortable and affordable home where Mr. Batzinger was able to sustain the development of its resources raise a family of 6 children, and even put them through college, despite the hardships brought on by the long labor strikes at General Electric in the 1950's and 1960's. The outline of the property, gardens and woods that Mr. Batzinger grew, can still be clearly seen, in the Google satellite view of the property.

While this picture brings back many fond memories of growing up in Guilderland, it also speaks of a time when development of a homestead from scratch was affordable and sustainable. This home was the product of a pay-as-you-go project done at a time when building codes and zoning laws did not add a significant expense to living off the land. For my generation, we did not realize it at the time but our chores not only contributed to the life of the family and we were learning how to live off the land. However, we have all moved away both from this house and from this lifestyle. Nonetheless, it is good to remember what it was like "back in the day." It is an approach to personal planning and development, useful and sustainable in all generations.

I should add an additional note about the mailbox in the photo. The snow load and wind-driven build up along Route 20 was considerable and the rural district of the county had many miles that had to be kept clear quickly. The resulting situation was a test of engineering and patience to come up with an inexpensive way to keep the mail box within the mail carrier's arm's reach from the road while protecting it from being buried or plowed over. After several failures, Dad settled on a design that had a strong base and an arm that could be easily repaired. He was proud that he had one of the largest and oldest mailboxes on the snowplow route. As one drives up and down Route 20, you will see many other good designs -- An old milk can base filled with cement that could be easily restored to its place, a long arm that allows the mailbox to swing away from the road as the plow hits, and other clever strategies.

However, despite the inconvenience of digging our driveway out after they passed by and the occasional need to restore the mailbox, our family always appreciated those road crews that worked around the clock to keep the roads clear even in the worst blizzards of the 1960's.

--- Robert Batzinger

Ma's Country store on Sharp's Corners
– restored and as it is in 2017

FULLERS

This is a designation of an area of Guilderland not frequently used. It got its name from Fuller's Station – it is the western edge of town past the reservoir, up to and including Fuller Station Road to the Duanesburg town line. The vintage photos above show houses in 1914 the railroad crossing over US route 20 as it was in 1935, just west of where the 84 Lumber Company is. Below is how they look in 2017.

As US 20 intersects state route 158 Ma's Service station stood. It was owned by Joe Calabro, but fell into ruin. It has been re-built, as Ma's Country Store and gas station. Route 158 north and south is still mostly rural showing Guilderland's roots. Along the south stretch however, once stood Dutcher's, a popular ice cream place.

THE VALE OF TAWASENTHA

As Altamont road (Route 146) moves south from Hartman's Corners, it's lined with homes dating back to the 1940s-50s and 60s. Just before the road crosses the Norman's Kill* - Inga Barth Flowers once stood. Just beyond the creek is a historic marker commemorating the Battle of the Norman's Kill. It then winds its way toward Guilderland Center.

The famous stream bearing its Dutch name passes around TAWASENTHA PARK on its way to the Hudson River.

Today, the park has pavilions, a pool, baseball fields, a winter recreation area, a creek side walk and foot bridge. Before that in the 1950's and early 60s it was quite different. Swimming was in the creek itself. Those who didn't care to pay the small park admission availed themselves of the creek on the other side of the bridge which was deeper and sported a rope hanging from a tree.

*See author's notes in the appendix.

As Doreen Reinemann, who lived only a mile away recalls -
"Going to Tawasentha before the pool was there, they had rides games and a snack bar down back. After the pool went in, we got to go swimming all day. On Friday nights, there were the Splash Parties so we went swimming, listened to bands and danced the night away. Fun times - that were the 1960's."

This photo from 2017 is as close as the author
can reckon that the original swimming area was.

Undated photos of the Tawasentha pool.

GUILDERLAND BABE RUTH

Tawasentha Park has long been the home of the Guilderland Babe Ruth League. Sitting high on the hill above the road, anyone who ever played or watched a game recalls - *"Please return all foul balls to the concession stand for a free freeze pop."*

1983 GUILDERLAND BABE RUTH GOP TEAM: Back Row (L-R) Charlie Brown, Steve Noel, Mike Baumann, Hodari Brooks, Andy Krauss, Eric Weideman, Ted Bastiani, Head Coach Green (Front Row L-R) Chris Ives, Al Evon, Chip Brown, Kevin Piazza, Bruce Bardin, Tony Parella, Butch Bastiani.

EASTWARD TO WILLOW STREET & BEYOND

Moving east from where his chapter began at Hartman's Corners, we must recall The Western Turnpike Golf course, The Bumble Bee Diner, The Mill Pond, M&M Motel, Willow Street and vicinity, Rose Hill, The Shadow Box, Guilderland Elementary School, Prospect Hill Cemetery and then on to the edge of Westmere.

Western Turnpike Golf Course - In 1929, the Realty Golf Corporation, the holder of two golf courses in the Albany area was forced to liquidate due to The Great Depression. The Stanford Golf Course, formerly located at the Mohawk Mall site, was turned over to its shareholders, while CEO Ned Vrooman held the Western Turnpike Golf Course. Around 1950 the course was turned over to the Szatkowski family to own and operate for over sixty years. In 2002 it was purchased by The Town of Guilderland.

Across from the entrance lived the Kipp family, including Ray and Myron adjacent to the Bumble Bee Diner. They were poor and their house with tarpaper siding shouted this out. It looked as if a strong wind would knock it over, but Ray was a hard worker and helped Mr. Andrews at the trailer court as well as Old Pop Carpenter. The Bumble Bee was a popular eatery for many years and later added the Bumble Bee car wash.

FOR SALE: The remains, now long gone,
and only photo of the Bumble Bee.

The Mill Pond came next with two creeks feeding it full of water that went down a spillway and under US 20 just west of Willow Street. Eventually, a road constructed bisecting it led to Mill Pond Acres, later Mill Pond Stables. The pond has long since, been overgrown with rushes and cattails.

Back in the day however, the Hunger Kill, which fed the pond ran well up and under Siver Road. It flowed through and around Charlie Gardner's property and Pine Haven Country Club. The Gardner family was big - Carole, Charlie Jr., Jim, Dave, Joan, Paul and Susan. Mr. Gardner worked for Tobin's First Prize. Mrs. Gardner worked just as hard tending to the family. Jim owned and operated the Altamont Enterprise. Paul began working at the age of 14 at the country club. He now resides in Pennsylvania and owns a string of propane and other companies including Heller's Gas. Of the family, the author knew Paul best because we met in Mrs. Morgan's kindergarten class in 1958. He taught me how to tie my shoes, which is why I now wear cowboy boots.

We spent countless hours tramping around in the woods and creeks near Siver Road. One March day, when we were still in elementary school, I was standing on the edge of the creek looking across. Paul pushed me in from behind. As I stood, water up to my knees and glaring at him – he jumped in. When I asked him why, he responded, "you looked so pissed-off, I figured you were going to push ME in. I thought probably it would be head-first. This way I won't get so wet."

Some years later, I told this story to my young son. When he asked to hear more stories, I realized that this was the only safe one to tell him – all the others had mischief of some kind.

The M&M Motel is still in operation. I was never sure what the M&M stood for but I reckoned Morier, because Albert and Henry Morier lived there. It was also the location of the historic Case Homestead. The historic marker is behind the inset in the photo above. It burned in 1950.

WILLOW STREET AND VICINITY

Before the glut of huge developments came to town along with monster houses and enormous lots, many residents lived along Western Avenue and up Willow Street or its tributary streets. Others lived off side roads like Foundry Road. The homes were older and more modest in size.

Above all, there was a sense of neighborhood and community. Kids rode their bikes or walked to friends homes. When they got into mischief (didn't many of us?) neighbors would often discipline them or report them to their parents. Games of street football or pick-up baseball games, hanging out in the basement or getting dirty in fields woods and streams was the norm. Was it perfect? Of course not, but it was real. It was our life, and that of our families.

Parents and other adults helped each other either with condolences for the loss of a loved one or fixing a leaky pipe. The following section will hopefully, conjure up those times.

Above are houses along the stretch on US 20 near Willow Street and of course the defunct Master Cleaners that served the community dry cleaning needs for decades. It is now awaiting environmental clean-up concerns.

Typical older, modest homes on Willow Street photographed in 2017. The one on the left was the home of Harold J. Warner Sr. His son of the same name, better known as "Butch."

Farther up Willow Street, long ranch houses began to spring up in the 1960's. These photos likewise, taken in 2017 as evidenced by the car on the right. Nonetheless, they are mostly unchanged.

Winters on Willow, as well as everywhere else in town were snowy and cold. This was the family home of Vicki Meade on Pinewood Drive. Snow blowers were yet to be common. Many made good but hard-earned dollars shoveling driveways.

When the author was five years old, he had to accompany his older brother, Vilko on just that type of job, albeit on Okara Drive. Our parents worked and he was the baby sitter. Repeated requests to the homeowner for "little brother" to stand in the foyer or garage because of the cold were refused. Halfway through the driveway, Vilko had to quit or see the author get frostbite. He was not paid, but I am grateful.

Located just north of Western Avenue on Willow Street, is the Guilderland State Police station, built in 1845. At that time, the building served as the first two-room school in town, the District 4 School on Willow Street. It had an average of 70 pupils in attendance. The teacher's pay was $1.50 per student for a school term of 72 days. Rebuilt in 1891, it was retired in 1953. It then served as the Town Hall until 1972. Today the historic building serves as the Guilderland State Police station.

On this same site, about 1800, was the one-room schoolhouse attended by Guilderland's famous author, Henry Rowe Schoolcraft. The young Schoolcraft was born two houses above the school site in the first two-story house in the settlement, then known as Dowesburg. Henry Schoolcraft was also a geologist, explorer, discoverer of the actual source of the Mississippi River, and expert on Native Americans.

The home of Henry Schoolcraft on Willow Street.

ROSE HILL (a.k.a. Dr. Lee's home and office)

This landmark, sited nearly in the middle of town on US 20 is Rose Hill, and has had just four owners in its existence, which probably accounts for its well-preserved state. Abraham Degraff, son-in-law of John Veeder, owned the mansion from 1880 until the turn of the century at which time, it was rented to tenants. In 1945, Dr. Miller Lee, a physician in general practice, bought the property. Then for the first time the house had water, electricity and plumbing facilities. The present owners, the Galonka Family, have kept the house in pristine condition. On the author's last visit in 2017, it was obscured by trees and not visible from the highway.

Old doctor Lee was bald as a cue ball but was damn sharp. He saved the author's father one day from a potentially fatal allergic reaction to a prescription from another doctor.

GUILDERLAND ELEMENTARY

Above is the school as it appeared in 1958. The goofy little boy is the author. It is still in the same location albeit with a traffic light to ease the tricky entrance. There are many class photos on the website but limited space here so there will only be a select few included. Virgil Sheeley was the Principal and Alton Farnsworth was the Superintendent for the district.

Many people opined that since Mr. Farnsworth was so tall, that was the reason for infrequent "snow days." If the snow was up to his knees, it was over most kid's heads. Bus numbers one through ten were still in service. Bus number three tipped over one day on Foundry Road because water covered the road and the ditch on the right side that it's wheels fell in. Another bus came to the rescue and the kids handed, one by one, to the new bus – the drivers standing knee deep in the flood.

Well-loved drivers like Sue Rosa, Olive Johnson or Ernie Saddlemire were at the wheel of some and knew us all by name.

From Sarah Johnson Moore - This was something given to my mom, Olive Johnson, I believe when she retired from driving school bus for Guilderland Schools. She drove from 1965 to 1982 I believe. She started when I was like three and she used to take me on the bus with her. Guess you could say that the bus was my babysitter of the day. Some of you might remember her as Mrs. Johnson and she had a Tweety-Bird on the front of her bus on the radiator. She drove many different routes but I know she did drive Altamont Hill and Willow Street.

SIDE BAR - To the best of the author's memory, some buses initially had cardboard or plywood in front of their grills – for what purpose I am clueless, but eventually many drivers painted them like Mrs. Johnson above, so little kids could identify their bus more easily as it came down the street.

If you look at the class sizes in the photos, note that there was one fabulous teacher for 24-26 kids – no assistants either!

1956-1957 Mrs. Gallitelli – Grade five and six! The author's brother, Vilko Green, GCHS class of 1963 is directly below the teacher.

1960 -1961- Good luck naming all of these people -
The author could only remember nineteen (himself included).

Teachers come and go in our school lives. - We have them for a year and move on but they often stay on for many years. Some move up to other levels and some stay on with the grades they know best. Some, no doubt whom we drove to distraction with our antics, retired or became hermits.

Above, left to right - Miss Carriere, Miss Palmer, Mrs. Parker, and Mrs. Tweedie.

Mrs. Tweedie was an avid bird watcher (yes, I can hear the chuckles) and organized morning "field trips" behind the school. Mothers came in to fix breakfast in the cafeteria and we all went out to find whatever avian friends we could find. The author never had French toast until the morning of the field trip.

Mrs. Tweedie however, didn't understand boys all that well. One day Paul Gardner and I were fighting on the playground when recess ended. She said, "Just go on fighting. The class is going back inside." - We did. A few minutes later, she came back out and shouted, "What are you doing?" While still fighting and rolling in the dirt we replied, "Just what you said to do." – *J. Green*

Mr. Dan Nicholas' 6th grade class:

BACK ROW – Carolyn McGinnis, Chris Aumic, Melissa Hale, Bob Davis, Roxanne Ballschmeieder, Harold Warner, Beverly Mackey, Craig Mengel, Annette Nadeau – Peter Kent, Leslie Mull, MIDDLE – Barb Laramore, Barb Exler, Chris Kaufman, Dorcas Gearhardt, Donna Kisby, Sue Robertson, Sharon Rapsard, Roberta Alger, Deborah Lockwood, Leslie Kenny, Ann Stuart FRONT – Jeff Gates, Jeff Auer, Ken Johnson, Leonard McHugh, Bill Stalker, Richard DeLeon, John Green, Dave Button, Richard Lane.

Mr. Nicholas later went on to be the Guilderland baseball coach However, once in class, the author told him that, "he didn't know what he was talking about." I was instructed to leave the room and await him in the hallway. He grasped me by the shoulders and gave me a firm push up into the lockers and said, "I never want to hear you tell me that again – understood?" I understood and he was my favorite teacher in elementary school. Imagine the outcome today.

PROSPECT HILL CEMETARY

Prospect Hill Cemetery has stood along Western Turnpike, now Western Avenue, as a visible part of the Guilderland community since it was founded in 1854. The grounds, which total over 50 acres, house the burial sites of many individuals whose names are prominent in the history of the Town, as well as several hundred military veterans whose service dates as far back as the War of 1812. Prospect Hill houses the remains of 161 veterans of the Civil War, and includes a "Soldiers Lot" and Gothic monument erected to memorialize veterans who served in that conflict. (Source: (www.ourtowneguilderland.com)

From Doreen Reinemann - My mom and dad are buried in Prospect Hill near my grandparents. When we went out to the playground at Guilderland Elementary, I use to sneak over to visit my grandparent's graves. I have a lot of family buried there. My grandmother died in March so she was in that building overlooking Western Avenue until spring that year.

LAST STOP IN GUILDERLAND

The corner of Route 155 (Karner Rd. to the north, State Farm Rd. to the south) and US 20 marks the beginning of Westmere, at least as far as this narrative is concerned. Karner Road was a dirt road for most of its length to Colonie. For a time, Rushin's Liquor Store and First National Bank of Scotia held down the NE corner, Robert Hall Clothes, the northeast. A&P dominated the southwest side and Star Plaza the southwest before the advent of 20 Mall or Hamilton Square as the whole area is known today. Star Plaza was owned, and managed by Savas (Sam) Ermides and the upper part is still owned by the Ermides family.

Originally an IGA (*International Grocers Association*), Star Market was the anchor to the plaza. In addition to this, Harry's Beef, Bottle and Beer (*later Doratos*), a drug store, dry cleaner and Guilderland Wine & Liquor. Above those were offices including D.J. Moore Advertising. Several of these will be mentioned in more detail below. The author notes that on his visit to Guilderland in May/June 2017 the only remaining original store is Guilderland Wine and Liquor.

RUDY'S GAS STATION, snack bar and cabins – 1939-1970 - owned by Fred & Emily Rudesheim, used to be where Dunkin Donuts is in Star Plaza on Western Avenue ran in late 1940s, 1950s, 1960s. A lot people called Fred, Rudy because is was short for his last name. My grandmother Carolyn graduated from GHS in 1958, one of the first graduating classes there. Carolyn passed away in 2010. She worked in the kitchen at Farnsworth Middle School from the early 1970s right up to the end of 2009-2010 school year. She passed in July 2010. – *Amanda LaForte*

RUSHIN'S LIQUOR STORE, was on the corner of Western Avenue and Karner Road where a Walgreen's is now. Stan and Helen moved the store there from downtown Albany because they were displaced by the construction of the Legislative Office Building of the Empire State Plaza, directly across State Street from the Capitol. They operated their store for many years at this location. Stan was also a member of the Western Turnpike Rescue Squad. He was often first on the scene when an accident occurred at their intersection. When Stan was robbed at gunpoint one evening, he ran out, unarmed, after the robber. A customer driving by saw him running, noticed a parked car running just around the corner behind Robert Hall and jotted down the license plate number. The robbers were arrested the next day on Long Island. - *Jim Rulison*

***

Joe Calabro who owned Joe's Service station on US route 20 at McCormack's Corners, came into Rushin's Liquor Store every few weeks and knew the proprietors Stan and Helen very well. During the oil embargo of the early 1970's, when there were long lines at the gas pumps and limits on how much gas one could purchase, Joe would close his station early and turn most of the lights out. He did, however, provide gas to his friends, like Stan and Helen and their employees, in those after hours so they wouldn't have to wait in line. I know- as an employee of Rushin's Liquor Store I was one of the beneficiaries of his actions. - *Jim Rulison*

HARRY'S BEEF BOTTLE & BEER owned by Harry Rucker was a popular eatery and watering hole for many years. Teachers from Farnsworth Middle School gathered there for cocktails, as did many business people, including employees of D.J. Moore Advertising and others in the Plaza. Mike Connelly was the assistant manager for many years and many of his bartenders and waiters are well remembered – Gloria, Jackie, Tess and Janice. Harry's was eventually replaced by Doratos restaurant.

One day, Sean Farley, (another art director), Kevin Russell, a paper sales representative for Hudson Valley Paper Company, and the author were being treated to lunch by a Mill representative, by the name of Jim Boulden. Jim was an ex-football player with a Rose Bowl ring and a daunting physique. Everyone ordered the same menu item, open face Italian sandwiches along with drinks. The sandwich portions were rather skimpy that day. When we finished eating our waitress, Janice, asked us if we wanted another round, thinking another round of drinks and trying to remember what everyone had. Three drink lunches were still common back then.

Jim said, "Yes, we would like another round – of lunches." He didn't complain and said he would pay for them. He had a generous expense account.

Harry, who was within earshot, heard him, and his face turned red. A few minutes later, a new round of sandwiches came to our table, this time heaped high with salami, tomato and cheese.

D.J. MOORE ADVERTISING.

Don Moore founded D.J. Moore Advertising in 1960 on Lark Street in Albany but moved to Guilderland sometime in the early 1970's. Through his writing and creative talent, he grew the company into one of the regions most recognized and respected advertising agencies. The agency closed in 2000. He continued to share his skills in retirement by doing pro bono work for the Teresian House and Community Caregivers. He was on the Board of Directors of A.I.A., The Ad Club, and was a past president of the Albany Country Club. He touched all he met with his generosity, wit and charm. He passed away in 2015 having influenced many lives, and being remembered as a true gentleman.

The author worked for him right out of college, as an art director from 1975-1985 learning more lasting lessons in four months with Don Moore than four years in college. We corresponded almost until his death and I dedicated one of my books, *"Confessions of a Graphic Prostitute"* to his memory. Harry's Beef Bottle & Beer was like a second office to the creative staff. Many an ad, or brochure concept, scribbled on a cocktail napkin.

Don Moore c. 1972 in his office with his typewriter

The author at the drawing board c. 1979

A GUILDERLAND GLIMPSES:

From Doreen Reinemann – Before the advent of huge companies like Waste Management, my father, Adam "Sonny" Reinemann, like many others, owned a rubbish removal business. He picked up trash for Guilderland schools and apartments in Guilderland and Westmere. Also The Village Drummer, Tommy Polito's Tavern, Bruce's Mobil Station, State Fair Bar & Grill, Thunderbird Pool and Driving Range, Town n' Country Lanes, Western Turnpike Golf Course, The Bavarian Chalet, Westlawn Lanes and many other businesses and private homes.

Candy Kraft gave him ribbon candy for our family at Christmas. I was so proud to be his daughter even when kids made fun of me because my dad was a rubbish man. But guess what? - If he didn't pick up their garbage they would have rats all over the place or would have to drive to the dump every week. It was honorable, hard work.

When my dad died, Tommy Polito came to his wake in 1997. When Tommy died, I went to show my respects to his family as he did to mine. They were both fine, hard-working men.

Doreen and father Adam Reinemann

The Farnsworth Middle School - 1969

Unknown soldiers – the author's guess – 1970's

Not Guilderland, but many of us went back and forth to the Turnpike and Carmen Drive and to this place - The Mohawk Drive-In. Opened in June 1946 - operated by Fabian Theaters. It closed in the 1980's and demolished on October 5, 1989. – *Jim Rulison*

FORT HUNTER

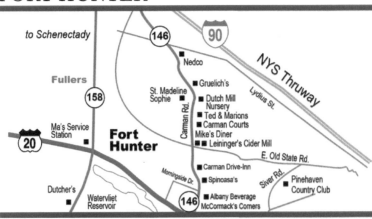

The core of the Fort Hunter area of Guilderland is Carman Road, and residential areas along Lone Pine, Spawn, Old State, Fuller Station Roads and Lydius Street. Businesses that used to line Carman Road are almost all gone. Mike's Diner is the lone exception and it has undergone major renovations. Spinosa's Market, The Carman Drive-in Theater, Leininger's Cider Mill, Greulich's Market, Ted & Marion's, Dutch Mill Nursery, DiCaprio's, and Nedco Pharmacy are gone – but not forgotten.

Encroaching on the older neighborhoods are the ubiquitous massive new homes and developments today, but many of the older homes remain.

Fort Hunter Elementary is long gone, replaced by Lynnwood and Pine Bush Elementary schools.

Despite the growth, areas of the Pine Bush, West Old State Road and Lydius Street remain wooded and secluded – *for now.*

Leininger's Cider Mill on Carman Road & Old State Rd. was *the place* to get fresh cider in the fall. By the cup or by the gallon! You could even bring your own container. It was on Old State Road just off Carman road.

This is the original Cider Mill. Carman Road is on the left, and it is going up towards the hill just before Sunset lane. It would have been about 1943. The woman in the light dress, in the center is Edith Leininger (my grandmother), and the last man on the left holding the Glass jug is Fred Warner, her brother. The actual history is that there was a cider mill on the property when they bought it. Eli Van Wagenen had owned and ran it. Many people came by and asked about the cider, so my grandfather decided at that time open one. *- submitted by Brian Leininger*

This is one of the most iconic images of the time. Along with the Turnpike, one of two drive-ins in Guilderland. "Don't let this happen to you," exclaimed the screen, warning of leaving the speaker in your car window when you left. "Only 2 minutes until show time," was the warning as they counted down while awaiting dark or after intermission. Screen messages also reminded you of the popcorn, burgers, hotdogs, and fries that awaited you at the concession stand. Some folks brought their own. Some brought beer. Some brought lawn chairs and blankets or lay down on the hood of their car. And of course, some never even watched the movie. They were usually found - parked way in the back.

The theater grounds are now occupied by
a housing development off Liberty Court.

While some worshiped celluloid celebrities, others worshipped another way. Saint Madeline Sophie was a church but also a Catholic School.

Before or after Church (*or even instead of church*), Mike's Diner was the place to go for breakfast or lunch.

The author once raised some serious eyebrows, years back, while visiting town wearing his usual Stetson, western shirt and cowboy boots. He exclaimed upon entering the diner, "I've come 3,000 miles for one of your hot dogs with meat sauce and onions. Come to think of it – make it two." They were as good as he remembered.

GREULICH'S MARKET

3403 Carman Road

Open Evenings and Sundays

Phone: EL 5-1530

Long before Price Chopper, Hannaford or the endless procession of super markets, there were neighborhood groceries like Greulich's. As Sonny & Cher opined, *"The grocery store's a super mart, uh huh..."* For many years however, Greulich's stayed in business with quality meats, local friendly service and even home delivery. The iconic cow was stolen and recovered many times too.

Greulich's Market - My dad worked in NYC when I was growing up, so my mom took care of everything in our household of four "women" - my mom and 3 girls. Only thing is, we didn't own a car. We ordered our groceries by phone (party line) from Greulich's. I remember a woody station wagon pulling up to our driveway with the boxes of groceries. Of course, back in those days there was not the fierce competition in pricing between markets. So much was delivered to the house - eggs, milk, bread (via Friehhofer's red truck of course). – *Aino Parlo*

A rare surviving class photo from Fort Hunter Elementary

This was from a parade going down Carman Road,
Fort Hunter elementary in the background, circa 1970.

TYPICAL HOMES ALONG CARMAN ROAD

This house is now a part of Dr. Tetreault's practice.
It is between the Medical Center and Mike's Diner.

Morningside Drive and Carman Road
formerly the Gogol home. Stan, Florence and Debbie.

Above - across from Carman Courts -
used to be the Harper Residence.

Carman Courts was one of three trailer courts in Guilderland.
The others were Andrews, and Magley's in McKownville.

"While looking through old photo albums I found this photo of Fort Hunter Fire Department, Dated 1981. I believe, this was the fire that started because a man drove his car into the Fire House. If memory serves, he fell asleep at the wheel. One of my Uncles was at the Fire Department when everything happened... Needless-to-say they were able to push the flaming car into the middle of the road before GFD arrived. – *anonymous*

In 1956 we moved into the house next to Dr. Arony's office. In our neighborhood, there were 35 kids to play with. Dr. Arony knew everyone and you couldn't get away with anything. I tried soaping the windows at Nedco Pharmacy one Halloween evening. Ripped my thumb open and had to go to him. He just *knew*, I didn't fall and cut myself - He just *knew*! I didn't do that again!

- Michelle Morini-France

A Fort Hunter story - Our family moved to West Lydius from Buffalo in 1971. In 1972 my Brother, Kevin came into the world. One day in 1976, he decided to take his big wheel on an adventure. After about an hour of frantic searching, we got a call from George Ginsburg at Nedco Pharmacy... "You missing a kid?" He had gone a half mile down Lydius, crossed Carman Road (just a stop sign then) and landed at Nedco. With a little detective work, George figured out who he belonged to. A great neighbor... that's how it was back then! Back around the same time, (74-76) I had a local paper route for the Gazette... I had to go 1/2 mile to the Getty station to pick up my papers... One February morning, the wind chill was nearly 30 below... As I was packing my bag in the numbing cold, a voice from the station said, "You want a coffee?" I never liked coffee to that point, but I said, "Is it hot?" From that day on, coffee made me feel good in the morning... that's also how it was back then...

---Patrick Walsh

On Carmen Road there was the Stutz Farm on the NW corner of Old State and Carmen. Just north of the Stutz Farm was a cold storage facility where folks could rent frozen lockers. Twice a year my dad would buy a side of beef and store it in the rented frozen locker. The Sunday ritual for my family in the 50's was to go to church at St Madeline Sophie, then pick up some frozen meat from the frozen locker and buy fresh vegetables from Stutz. In the late 60's home freezers became quite affordable and with the opening of the new hydroelectric facilities the price of electricity dropped to the point that we no longer needed to rent a frozen locker.

- *Robert Batzinger*

As a side bar, Mr. Stutz -a.k.a. "Bumpy" would attach a plow to one of his trucks and plow snow during the winter months. The Stutz Farm is long gone today.

AMBUSH ON CARMEN ROAD

One day in the late 60s after school, my neighbor on Okara Drive, Robert Klein and I decided to take a bike ride up Carmen Road. We went up Okara, past Draper Pharmacy, where I had once bought batteries by light from flashlights during the great Northeast blackout, then took a right up Carmen Road. We continued on past Spinosa's little store where our neighbor Marie Vitale worked and continued on past Byers trucking on the left to Old State Road , there was no light there then. I don't know if the Cider Mill was still on the corner at that time, but we could see the Stutz farm and the many farm fields. We rode a little further passing a small farm field on our right when suddenly splat, I took a solid hit from a rotten tomato. More rotten tomatoes flew our way and I could hear the farmer "Bumpy" Stutz laughing as we pedaled away as fast as we could. (I played softball at the time with

Bumpy and his son Keith on the Lynwood Reformed Church team). I was covered with rotten tomatoes and seeds.

Not willing to let things sit, we came sneaking back to where the small farm field intersected a side road off Carmen and each gathered a good handful of tomatoes while "Bumpy" was busy working in the field. We got as close as we could on our bikes and then let go a time on target long-range barrage in "Bumpy's" direction. When they started landing he came charging toward us shouting and throwing tomatoes as he came. We hopped on our bikes and pedaled off as fast as we could. Now we were the ones laughing, although I doubt any of our tomatoes found their mark. The fields are gone now, all built up, last I knew Rob was a PHD with the DEA in DC. He told me that the army had later offered him a captaincy and a chance to be on their Olympic shooting team. He was a good shot at Watervliet Fish and Game Club, but luckily, he turned it down as the Olympics were canceled that year. –Jay Mohr

FOND FORT HUNTER MEMORIES by Anita Lopez –

One thing I remembered about Fort Hunter Elementary was during the Christmas season, there was a tree in the front lobby. We would bring in presents to be put under the tree. They were for the Children's Home in Schenectady. I really enjoyed doing that and I looked forward each year to putting a gift under the tree.

My kindergarten class was the first one to have class in the new classroom. As you walked in the main door, past the office, straight ahead you would see Mrs. Baldauf waiting for us. The first half of the year, we were in the basement, which later became the art room. I used to hate going down those stairs. My brother, Mark would walk me down the hall to the stairs and make sure I got safely downstairs. I would then sneak back upstairs and chase after him. Kathy Adamczak taught me to tie my shoes. And I loved eating the white school paste. Fingerprinting on paper plates was fun too. Our kindergarten class is the one on the Fort Hunter page.

Another favorite pastime of mine was going in the hall and cleaning erasers. That was lots of fun, as was the library. Right before school ended in June, you could take books out to read during the summer. One thing I miss about elementary school was getting my free tickets for the Altamont Fair. There was always something to look forward to.

***

My mom, Olive Johnson, started driving bus in 1967. It started being for just one year, just until my dad went back to work. GE was on strike, so mom decided to learn how to drive a bus. When September rolled around, it was "just one more year." That would continue until 1981 or 1982.

She had many adventures in her driving career. On one of her kindergarten runs, she ended up having a little boy travel around with her long after he was supposed to be dropped-off. She bought him lunch, checking back with the bus garage frequently to see if the mother had called. Turned out the mother forgot he was not going to the babysitter's and instead went to lunch with a friend.

Another time, while driving in Altamont, kids were laughing in the back of the bus. My mother, not being one to tolerate a lot of racket, asked what the problem was. One of the boys said, "Someone is back here, I think she might be in labor!" Mom stopped the bus and went back to check it out. Sure enough, some girl was in labor. She shooed all the boys up front. I think she tried to make sure the girl was comfortable. I don't remember if she delivered the baby or not, I think she may have. I *do know* that the girl's mother was in for a shock when a big yellow bus stopped in front of her house. My mother informed her that her daughter just had a baby, and for her to come see for herself.

Many kids I know rode my mom's bus. She was not one to pull punches when it came to behavior. She often assigned seats, and take away riding privileges. She didn't care who you were, or who your parents were. But, she has also zipper up coats, and buttoned the back of a shirt for a little kindergartner. As much as I loved my mom, I didn't like riding her bus. My siblings and I were held to a higher standard. There was NO getting away with anything on her bus - *especially* if you were her kid. By the time she retired, she was also teaching new drivers. Even after she retired she was *still* being asked to teach the new drivers.

Mom went into a nursing home, and would tell her stories about her driving days. Every time she told the story, she would add more years as to how long she drove. Soon, family members of the other residents could tell her stories as they had heard them so often. Mom died in 2010, three weeks prior to my 35-year reunion.

A favorite childhood memory was going to the Fort Hunter Fire Department about a week before Thanksgiving, for their annual "Turkey Raffle" fundraiser. The fire trucks parked out front and inside, rows of long tables soon filled to overflowing with friends and neighbors. Baskets of potato chips and pretzels put out along with pitchers of beer and soda -- at no charge! Up front was a huge wheel of chance and tables filled with the night's prizes. Firemen went around selling tickets for, I believe, a quarter apiece and for each round of tickets, the wheel was spun three times. The first lucky winner got a frozen turkey, the second a bottle of liquor and the third, a bottle of wine. The festivities ended when all the prizes had been won, and we walked to our cars in the crisp late autumn air, laden with turkeys and booze. Many times, we got our first dusting of snow that evening, much to the delight of us kids -- a fun start to the holiday season! – *Deborah Gogol Deer*

WESTMERE

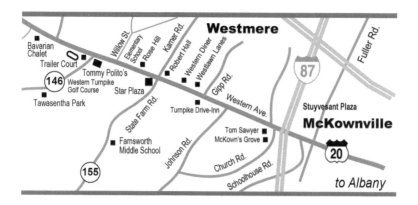

Westmere and McKownville grew faster than the more rural western part of Guilderland because of their proximity to Albany. As with the rest of the town, Western Avenue (US 20) was the business center. Robinson & Hennett, Zimmerman's Shell, The Turnpike Drive-In, Westlawn Lanes, Western Diner & Motel, Westmere News, Caruso's, Manor House, Mikes/Neba, Walt's Subs, Central Market, White Eagle Bakery, Turnpike Rescue Squad, Dairy Queen, Tina Marie's, Marty's Fish Fry, Farmer in the Dell, The Penguin and countless others. Residential areas flourished off major side streets such as Church, Gipp, Johnston and Schoolhouse Roads.

The Western Diner is still cooking - the exterior photo is vintage but the inside is contemporary. The author ate there in 2011 and 2017 during a visit from his home in Arizona.

The Western Diner opened in 1978, the owner of Dusand's a restaurant on Rt. 155, was the owner, with his wife Donna, along with their son Doug. The original inside was yellow gold and every booth had a jukebox. -- *Joy Cotazino*

Westlawn Lanes was right down the road. Approximately cross from the Turnpike Drive Inn.

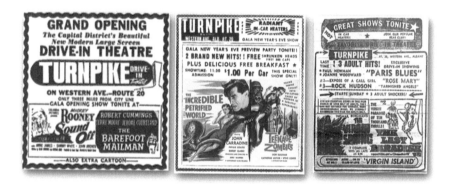

There is no photo existing of the old Turnpike Drive-in Theater, but these ads should stir some memories. The original builder/owner was John Gardner. It was operated by Alan Iselin. The Turnpike opened in August, 1952 and closed in 1983. Highwood Village Residential Housing now occupies the lot.
--- *Sheree Notaro*

Many may remember the Turnpike having a playground in front of the screen where children played while waiting for dark. Whole families brought lawn chairs, blankets and picnic baskets. Men may remember the "latrine-style" bathroom where all stood in front of a long open sink to do their business.

Who can forget the "Home of the Club Burger? They also offered thick shakes, fish sandwiches, French fries or *Looney-Toon* collectible glasses that were really glass! Carrols was later turned into Burger King franchises.

This photo, taken in 2017 is of the
original Westmere News and Deli.
that the new owner preserved.

Sledding in the Pine Bush between Velina and Victor Drive. There was also a shack that housed construction equipment at the bottom. A much larger dune was behind Velina where the Lupien's and Boynton's lived in the late 1950's and 60's. These were leveled and are now single-family homes on the extended part of Velina Drive.

Fires in the Pine Bush used to be common. There was no town water, so the Rulison's kept a hose on their well to stop any embers from spreading the fires. They were also allowed to help the Westmere FD tackle fires with backpack hand pumped water tanks. Something that OSHA would have a conniption fit about today!

Below is 33 Velina Drive - Westmere - This photo shows a 1959 Chevy wagon, what families toted the families in before the mini van! - *Jim Rulison.*

Caroline's Railroad - off Gipp Road.

WESTMERE ELEMENTARY SCHOOL
Mr. James Cleary, Principal

Mr. Pinto - Grade 3
1978   1979

A rare vintage photo of Westmere Elementary.
Mr. Cleary was the Principal but was originally the vice Principal
at Guilderland Elementary.

Vintage Western Avenue homes

My grandfather, Howard Westervelt, whom most people called "Pop," sold fruits, vegetables, flowers and other produce from his road stand on Schoolhouse Road. He also grew peanuts. People came from as far as New York City to buy what were then called "new potatoes." My father Adam, raised pigs there too.

I went to Westmere Elementary, until the 3rd grade when we moved to route 146 (Altamont Road) in Guilderland just below route 20. I hated to leave Schoolhouse Road. There was a hill in the back of our house. We could sled down right into our back door. There was also a little store nearby where we got penny candy and jelly doughnuts on Sundays. I guess you could say my heart belonged to Schoolhouse Road. ---*Doreen Reinemann*

In the early 60's the town of Guilderland sponsored Saturday evening "Canteens" at the Westmere Elementary School. I remember it was 25 cents to enter. Soda and Pizza were sold. Mostly it was music and dancing in the gym, but there were board games in a few hallways,

Walkers were not encouraged - parents asked to drop off students and return to pick them up. If you left the canteen, you could not return.

My friends and I were at the Canteen the night that Butchie Bastianni, his brother and 2 others left the Canteen - walking to get refreshments other than pizza and soda. They were walking along Western Ave. Butchie was struck and killed by a hit and run driver. It was a major trauma for all that night. Systems were not in place in those days to help kids deal with the trauma. It was really a difficult time for many. - *Sherry Birdsey Chilton*

First National Bank of Scotia – owned by the Burmaster family, is still there. The author had his first checking account there in 1971. When he visited in 2011, little had changed, even the paintings inside.

This photo needs no caption does it?

McKOWNVILLE

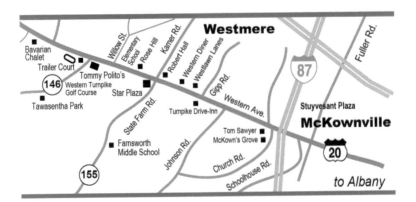

McKownville is named for John McKown and family, early settlers from the 18th century. Its school closed in 1953, replaced by Westmere Elementary. Originally, the gateway to the west from Albany, it tends to blend into the city of Albany but has a very distinct identity, especially to the baby boomer generation. Stuyvesant Plaza, which was the first suburban shopping plaza built outside Albany is still one of the retail anchors of the area.

Stuyvesant Plaza

Stuyvesant Plaza is the 2nd oldest shopping center in the Capitol District. Some of the older stores included: - Denby's - Western Auto - Flah's - Ormond's - Grand Union - Record Town - McManus & Riley - Golden Krust Bakery - Mechanics and Farmers Bank - Richman's Card Shop - W.T. Grant & Co. - Woolworth's - Hall's Drug Store, Cowen & Lobel, *Can you name more?*

c. 1969

...and of course, right in front of Stuyvesant Plaza was Howard Johnson's Restaurant with its *28 Flavors of ice cream!* "Ho-Jo" was the place to go - especially for their all-you-could eat specials – chicken, fish or spaghetti. Once, the Guilderland High School baseball team descended on them and had a chicken eating contest. Geoff Broom won by eating twenty-one pieces and Howard Johnson discontinued the deal for quite some time after.

The Tom Sawyer Motor Inn was high-end accommodations for its day. It also had restaurant and banquet facilities. The business that later located next to it was aptly named - Huckleberry Finn!

HOPPERS BAR

I was thirteen the first time I went in with my dad. He ordered a shot and a beer for himself and a beer for me. The woman behind the bar said, "I don't think he's old enough". My dad replied, "If my son wasn't old enough I wouldn't have brought him in." I was never proofed again. - *submitted by Stephen Curran*

"Myself and a few of my friends were regulars at Hopper's by the time we were juniors at Guilderland (1967). Great clams, cheap beer and endless games of pool. I seem to remember the owner's name was Abe. I can't remember his wife's name but she was a character too! We lived in Altamont and would sometimes take the afternoon bus there after school and hitchhike home around 4:00 to get home in time for dinner! Friday and Saturday nights were always fun at Hopper's too."--*submitted by Lou Hall.*

McKownville Fire Dept.

McKown's Grove was a popular family gathering place for swimming, picnics and just hanging out.

GRAND OPENING

JIM BULLOCK
Dealer

LEN WAGER
Day Attendant

PAUL ANZALONE
Night Attendant

1254 WESTERN AVE. – McKownville

O'Hanlon's Mobil

The Toll Mansion on Krumkill Road

GUILDERLAND CENTER

For most of the baby boomer generation, Guilderland Center is best known as the location of Guilderland Central High School. It was a small hamlet unto itself long before that. Guilderland Center was originally called by the locals "Bang-all," in reference to ill effects and reputation that rum, horse-racing, and the rough manners of the place brought. Around 1803 when the town of Guilderland formed, the name Guilderland Center began to come into fashion and by 1866, the hamlet had a population of four hundred-fifty persons.

The US Army Depot (later to become Northeast Industrial park), Helderburgh Reformed Church and the Guilderland Center Firehouse were also there long before a teacher stepped into a classroom or a cheerleader on a football field.

This is the corner of route 146, before the left turn to the high school. Empie's was across the street - now a gas station. "Go Dutchmen" may have been the football fight song, but "Meet me at Empies" meant another kind of fight was brewing.

Houses on Main Street that have been there for generations.

The historic Frederick House built in 1802.

Originally St. Marks, Lutheran, in 1872,
then Berean Baptist, then Helderburgh Reformed Church –
It is now yet another denomination in 2017

Guilderland Central High School
GUILDERLAND CENTER, NEW YORK

GUILDERLAND CENTRAL HIGH SCHOOL
Constructed in 1953 with additions and upgrades added in 1955, 1959, 1965, 1997, and 2009.

...as it was and... as it is today – at least for now.

In this section we will take a quick glance at the school but with only selected photos because just one yearbook would be prohibitive to reproduce. Besides, the author only has a few. All are now available in the internet via sites like Classmated.com. Hence, the focus will be on faculty that has been around for quite some time and as general photographs as possible. If your favorite, or not so favorite person is not included, the author apologizes in advance.

Charles Ciaccio – Dorothy Jenner – Mary Ryan – Dolores Ropke

Bud Kenyon – Fred Field – Don Snyder – Herm Wyld

The above, like 'em love 'em or hate 'em were chosen for their long tenure. Principal Ciaccio was there since roughly the Spanish-American War – As for Mrs. Jenner and Mrs. Ryan – if you didn't like them you were unpleasable. The coaches were football, baseball, soccer and wrestling respectively.

Football always draws the most people and attention. I will leave it to some readers to decipher the numbers and the players. The chilly cheerleader on the far right Sue Siebert, was chosen because she was a sweet soul and sadly, recently passed away in 2013.

Team Members: Row 1: D. Blagriff, T. Miltner, J. Bess, R. Engel, M. Garno, H. Baumes, M. Robinson, D. Pidgeon. Row 2: R. Berschwinger, P. Gallub, J. Clark, G. Lauver, C. Finn, D. Shuff, D. Berschwinger. Row 3: M. Kane, B. Cain, J. McClellan, J. Carusone, B. Southwood, J. Green.

1969- 1970 Guilderland Baseball Team – some here never made the team. Because of the way yearbooks were structured, spring sports were published the following year.

Not from any yearbook – the author found and appropriated the above photo from the yearbook out-take box in 1970. The on-deck batter shown coaching home plate as taught by JV Coach Alan Sholtes, is the author. Charlie Finn is attempting to score. Note the batter's bat is also in hand to avoid injury to catcher and runner.

Of course, GCHS is known for great teachers, sports and a host of other activities but this is straight out of research on Wikipedia:

Guilderland High School is also known for its theatre program. The group, called the Guilderland Players, was organized in the 1968-69 school year by English teacher Bob Scrafford, but did not put on their first performance, Bye Bye Birdie, until the next year. Musicals were directed for many years by the inimitable Fred Heitkamp. Producing two shows each year, a drama in the fall and a musical in the spring, the Guilderland Players, known as 'GP' by its members, is one of the largest extracurricular activities at Guilderland High School, including more than one hundred students in its cast, stage crew, and pit. It is staffed by Alexis St. Clair (Pit Conductor), Rae Teeter (music director), and Andy Maycock (director). The Guilderland Players' 2006 production of Steel Pier won the SLOC Award for 'Best Choreography.' Various alumni of the Guilderland Players have also gone on to other acting opportunities, including appearing on the TV show American Dreams, the Original Broadway Cast of La Bohème, and in the cast of multiple seasons of Park Playhouse.

Clockwise from upper left: Fred Heitkamp, South Pacific 1978, Guys and Dolls, 1972, Damn Yankees 1973.

The Pajama Game - 1971

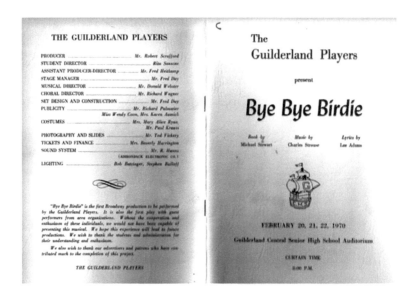

From the archives – 1970 Guilderland Players Bye Bye Birdie program.

GUILDERLAND CENTRAL'S FIRST GRADUATING CLASS HOLDS REUNION — Seventeen graduates of Guilderland Central High school's class of 1955 attended the 20-year reunion held last Saturday at the Americana Hotel in Colonie. Front row (from left): John Ryan, Gladys O'Brien (Miss Kniskern), Mary Alice Ryan (Miss Sutter), Delores Ropke, Charles Ciaccio, all teachers or advisors to the class. Second row: Joanne Moody (Gerard), Carolyn Hoskyns (Davis), June Salsbury (McNicoll), Shirley Lowe (Lochner), she came up from Florida, Persis Vehar (Parshall). Back row: Joseph Petrosino, Frank Elliott, Howard Jacobson, James Gardner, Leonard Ditton, James Canavan, King Clement, LeRoy Whinnery, Bernard Stahl, Thomas Prout, David Ward, Martin Markessinis. The class is looking forward to another reunion in 10 years. Photo by Bob Baldauf

Class of 1958 reunion.

"Kumbaya" - The '70's – Debbie Gogol
Nancy Gertzberg (deceased 2014) and Lin Harper

Of course, like any good little burg, there were a few bars and Taverns. Dells, just outside of town, The Cell Lounge, later to become the Late 'n' Lazy run by Ken Wesolowski.

One lonely New Years Eve, the author joking said to Kenny,
"Whiskey barkeep, and leave the bottle!" A bottle of Jack Daniels'
was placed in front of him on the bar and left there all night
– no charge.

STORIES FROM "BACK IN THE DAY"

Baseball was my main passion, but I dabbled with other things like wrestling, indoor track and football. The third string of the football team of which I was a permanent member, was scrimmaging the first team one afternoon and the first team ran a right end sweep. Ken Johnson our halfback, broke right through and was heading rapidly for the end zone. Playing right defensive cornerback, I started to give chase from the far side of the field. Running down Kenny from behind, he rode him down facemask first into the dirt with a shoulder high tackle. That was satisfying enough, but later after practice my friend Bruce Weber told me that two coaches were taking bets on whether I would catch him or not. Coach Steenburgh won the bet. – *the author*

***

I loved baseball and had since I was six years old. I was always the first on the field and the last one off. I led the team runs and always pitched batting practice. I was not however, the star of the team. To my surprise, just before graduation, Coach Field came up to me and thanked me for my hustle and keeping the team on its toes all season. We reached the sectionals again and I still vividly remember the last inning of the eleven-inning game against arch rivals Scotia High. Trailing by a run, I came to the plate with two outs. Cocky John Eggleston, whom I knew and already disliked from my childhood summers in Scotia, playing baseball while staying with his grandmother, was on the mound. Since I was in the number eight slot in the line up, he apparently felt very confident. The first pitch was a called strike. I thought it was low, so in addition to not wanting to make the last out, I was now pissed off to boot. The next pitch, a fastball down the middle, flew off my bat into the gap in left center field. The outfielders were still chasing it as I approached second base. As I sped toward third, Mark Garno was giving me the "hold up" sign, his hands in the air like I was under arrest. Being the team player I was, I held up at third. On every subsequent pitch, I hoped for a wild pitch or passed ball and even contemplated trying to steal home. The batter struck out on three pitches and that ended what was to be the last game I ever played in. – Many decades later, another teammate, Mike Kane opined through Facebook: "I would have sent him." -- *the author*

ALTAMONT

Altamont, although part of the town of Guilderland, is a more self-contained entity, because of its geographic isolation from the other sections of town. The Village has certainly changed over the years and has some businesses like restaurants, a Funeral home and Altamont Orchards, its historic heritage has little changed. It remains a quiet village.

In colonial times, this area was part of the Manor of Rensselaerwyck, granted by the Dutch West India Company to Killian Van Rensselaer in 1630. The area was known as Hellerburgh in the early 18th century. This settlement eventually became known as Altamont.

Altamont was a summer vacation spot reached by train. The station stop is now the location of the Altamont Free Library. The Altamont Fair has been held annually in the local fairgrounds since 1893.

Above is an aerial view of the Altamont Fair in 1957.
Below is as it might have appeared at any time.

The Appel Inn Bed and Breakfast at Route 146 and 158.
Originally Henry Appel's Tavern from the 1760's

The Altamont Manor – now a wedding venue.

Breitenback Castle on Route 146.

In 1976, Breitenbach began constructing by hand a small castle, on land given him by his father In 1987 he added a large studio addition. Breitenbach quarried stones (some as long as 12 feet) from a nearby creek, cut trees for lumber, and salvaged a collapsing carriage barn for beams and siding. He forged iron hardware, made leaded-glass windows, furniture, carvings, tile work, and a fresco, so that many of the arts could be represented. He intends to leave the castle and paintings behind as a museum. - *source: wikipedia*

For more information: http://www.tebreitenbach.com

Fredendall Funeral Home

On the way to Altamont on route 146

ALTAMONT STORIES

Has any one been on the Old Indian Ladder Trail to Thatcher Park recently? The trailhead used to be at the town limits for Altamont on Route 156. The first part was covered in poison ivy but after the first 100 feet, the path was easy walking and well worn. I often enjoyed this hike to Thatcher with friends, as it was a journey back in time. Lloyd Sharp (the youngest of the Sharps at Sharps Corner) used to tell stories of summer day camps organized by the YMCA's and YWCA's of Schenectady and Albany counties to take city kids on a hike to Thatcher Park back in the day when the railroad brought people for their vacations to Altamont. Even in the 1970s, the cliff faces along the trail still had whitewashed advertisements for old medicinal remedies and horse and buggy accessories of the 1920s. Trees had since grown in obstructing the view of these cliff faces but the trail must have had a lot of use by lots of little feet, as it was still visible with very few trees growing in the packed soil of the pathway. With all the development of that area and safety barriers added to Thatcher Park I wonder if anyone has been on that trail and if the advertisements are still visible. - *Robert Batzinger*

Altamont - Halloween 1964 or 1965 - Guilderland High School students came from all over. About 30 or 40 of us split up on either side of Main Street by the old A&P. We pretended to be pulling a rope like tug of war across the street to see what the cars would do. Some stopped, some didn't and some had some "kind" words do us. - *Bernie Erwin*

AFTERWARD

To all readers: Every reasonable attempt has been made to insure and verify the accuracy of events and places. Contributor's entries have been taken at face value with no judgment but many thanks. Some like Bob Batzinger, wrote lengthy articles, and many, like Doreen Reinemann contributed quite a few short passages. As and old advertising man, one of my favorites came from Jim Purtell – "I used to call it the bar that made Nieliwocki famous," in regards to The Village Drummer and referencing Schlitz Beer's famous slogan.

Any discrepancies or errors are completely the responsibility of the author and perhaps his memory faded over time. If it is any consolation to me, Stephen King, a more prolific and an immensely more successful author than myself included in his famous book, *The Stand*, a passage where a group of apocalyptic survivors camped overnight in Guilderland along route 80/90. Perhaps he might have consulted a map, as there is no such route or road, as you all know.

It is my fervent hope that you have enjoyed this book and the trip down memory lane. Since many writers "write what we know," you might enjoy two of my fictional books, *Roadside 66* and *The Elephant in the Room,* both of which make brief visits to Guilderland. And of course, *Tommy Polito's Tavern,* which is a semi-fictional story with a rather Twilight Zone type ending but makes a similar trip down memory lane based on a trip the author made to Guilderland in 2011 to visit his dying father.

APPENDIX

ACKNOWLEGEMENTS

Thanks to all who contributed stories, anecdotes and photographs. Some came through the website and others from a private Facebook page entitled: "You Know You're from Guilderland When..."

Contributors:

- Jim Rulison
- Doreen Reinemann
- Anita Thiela-Green
- Jay Mohr
- Ron Furbeck
- Jeff Orsini
- Michelle Morini France
- John LaJeunesse
- Brian Leininger
- Dan Nieliwocki
- Joy Cotazino
- Robert Mosall
- Kathleen Ashline
- Lou Hall
- Don Albright
- Debbie Gogol Deer
- Sarah Johnson Moore

- Robert Batzinger
- Rudolf Zwicklbauer
- Leslie Anne LaGuardia
- Bernie Erwin
- Carl Burnham
- Gayle Gifford
- Terry Miltner
- Joy Cotazino
- Amanda LaForte
- Patrick Walsh
- Sheree Notaro
- Joe Losito
- Aino Parlo
- Stephen Curran
- Jim Purtell
- Anita Lopez
- Sherry Birdsey Chilton

Authors Note: Throughout this book, I have referred to the Norman's Kill using the original name – Dutch for Norman's Creek. Often people call it Normanskill Creek, which is rather redundant. The area, originally settled by the Dutch in colonial times bears many Dutch names. The author finds it humorous that in his time Italian last names were predominant in the general population.

ABOUT THE AUTHOR

John F. Green is originally from Guilderland, NY -GCHS class of 1971. He lived in town from 1957 to 1984 near the corner of Altamont Road and US route 20, until moving to Rotterdam.

Moving to Arizona in 1999, he eventually retired as a graphic designer, advertising art director, copywriter and illustrator. His career can be seen here: www.creativecolleagues.com

He now spends half his time now at his 40 acre off the grid ranch in northern Arizona, occasionally joined by his lovely and forbearing wife Wendy. Many of his stories are written there during the quiet starry nights amid the howls of coyotes, hooting owls and things that go bump in the night.

For more information, and other books by this author including his best selling novella, *"Tommy Polito's Tavern,"* please go to:

www.jgreenbooks.com

OTHER BOOKS BY J. FRANKLIN GREEN

Young Readers:
- THE WIND IN THE JUNIPERS -

Apocalyptic Fiction:
- THE ELEPHANT IN THE ROOM -

Science Fiction:
- ALIEN HEREDITY -
- AND THE MEEK SHALL INHERIT -

Historical Fiction:
- IMMORTAL SERGEANT BACHMAN -

Recovery:
- BOOZE & BETRAYAL -

Supernatural Suspense:
- ROADSIDE 66 -
- TOMMY POLITO'S TAVERN -

Non-Fiction:
- CONFESSIONS OF A GRAPHIC PROSTITUTE –

- EVERYTHING I NEEDED TO KNOW ABOUT LIFE,
I LEARNED ON A BASEBALL FIELD
(*Well, Almost*) –

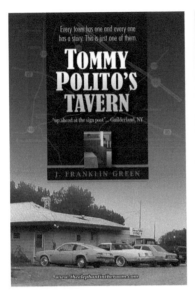

"Up ahead at the sign post..."

They say you can never go back and maybe you shouldn't. Thirty-two years after he left his hometown, Jonathan Moran returns to visit his dying father and spends a long afternoon driving down "memory lane" only to find a portal to the past and maybe a date with destiny.

This is a story of a town the way it was and never will be again. And a tavern like thousands of others across America that shaped many a memory and many a life.

www.jgreenbooks.com